Contents

Introduction v

1. Tithing 3
2. The Reward Passages on Tithing 21
3. Woo Hoo! It's All Mine! 33
4. Cheerful Stewards of God's Money 43
5. Grace to Those Who Differ 69

   Bibliography 73

*Spirit-Led Giving through
New Testament Stewardship*

The *Cheerful* Giver

John Orla

The Cheerful Giver
by John E. Orla

© Copyright 2020 by John E. Orla. All rights reserved.

Unless otherwise indicated, scripture quotations are taken from
The Holy Bible, New King James Version.
Copyright © 1982 by Thomas Nelson, Inc.
All rights reserved. Used by permission.

Scripture quotations marked (NIV) are from
The Holy Bible, New International Version®, NIV®.
Copyright © 1973, 1978, 1984 by Biblica US, Inc.®
All rights reserved. Used by permission.

Scripture quotations marked (NASB) are from
The Holy Bible, New American Standard Bible.
Copyright © 1960, 1962, 1963, 1968,
1971, 1972, 1973, 1975, 1977, 1995
by The Lockman Foundation, La Habra, Calif.
All rights reserved. Used by permission.

Without limiting the rights under copyright reserved above, no part of this publication — whether in printed or ebook format, or any other published derivation — may be reproduced, stored in or introduced into a retrieval system, or transmitted, in any form or by any means (electronic, mechanical, photocopying, recording or otherwise), without the prior written permission of the publisher.

The scanning, uploading, and distribution of this book via the Internet or via any other means without the permission of the publisher is illegal and punishable by law. Please purchase only authorized electronic editions and do not participate in or encourage electronic piracy of copyrightable materials.

Publication Design & Management:

lamppostpublishers.com

Published by:
John E. Orla
johneorla@gmail.com

ISBN-13: 978-1-60039-126-2 (Trade Paperback)

INTRODUCTION

A few years ago my wife and I attended a twelve-week Christian-based finance seminar. As we sat in a church gymnasium with thirty other couples, we received great advice on how to get out from under the "crushing weight of debt."[1] Some of us even cried as we began to have hope that we could actually conquer our finance troubles without having to resort to bankruptcy or home foreclosure. Each of us listened carefully and took meticulous notes.

Then, near the end of the twelve weeks we were thrown a curve ball. While learning how to create a budget and pay down our credit cards, our instructor surprised us by saying we needed to add a new financial obligation to our spreadsheet. He said it was necessary for each of us to calculate

---

1 Dave Ramsey, *Dave Ramsey's Financial Peace University Workbook* (Brentwood: The Lampo Group, 2008).

10 percent of our monthly income and give it to our local church, which is called a "tithe."[2] My reaction was quick and confused. *Hey, I thought this seminar was about getting out of debt and now you're telling me I have a debt to God?* He said his own pastor had showed him several Bible verses which clearly teach that all believers are required to give a tithe and by doing so *in faith* God would reward us with greater blessings.

He quoted Malachi 3:10 as proof of this Bible teaching:

> "Bring all the tithes into the storehouse,
> That there may be food in My house,
> And try Me now in this,"
> Says the Lord of hosts,
> "If I will not open for you the windows of heaven
> And pour out for you such blessing
> That there will not be room enough to receive it."

He then gave us several examples of how people received blessings, including financial independence, for meeting this monetary obligation to the church. One of the most convincing examples was his own testimony. He too used to be overwhelmed by debt, but now he is a multi-gazillionaire. He was very convincing and I started thinking through my own scenario, "If I paid the church 10 percent, then God would give me more money in return? That doesn't sound like debt, that sounds like a good investment strategy!"

---

2 ibid

INTRODUCTION

During the next five years, fully convinced we should give a tithe, my wife and I started giving *more* to the church. However, we never quite made it to 10 percent. To be honest, we didn't even get close. We just didn't have that much to give. With two adults and four children living on a single government service income in one of the highest priced home markets in the country (The San Francisco Bay Area), I couldn't afford a $200 car payment; how in the world was I going to pay $500 per month to the church?

When I told a Christian brother I couldn't tithe because I didn't have enough money to do it, he laid on the guilt.

"The reason you don't have enough to give is because you haven't given enough."

What?

"If you take the step of faith and give a full 10 percent, God will bless you with the money to make ends meet. God is obligated to provide abundantly, more than you could ever imagine."

I argued, "But if I gave even 5 percent of my monthly income to the church, for just one month, we wouldn't have enough money left over to eat."

"I used to think that," my friend said. "But I gave my tithe anyway. The next day there was a bag of groceries on my porch from an anonymous person, with a note that read, 'God told me to give this to you.'"

I believed him, but I felt like I was standing on the edge of a cliff and God was saying, "Don't worry. I'll catch you. Jump, John, jump!" But I couldn't bring myself to do it.

Whenever I saw the financial officer at the church, I walked the other way, convinced he was shaking his head inside. He probably wasn't thinking of me at all, but I was filled with shame. I was sure everyone knew about this appalling sin and was judging me for it.

Then one evening in Bible College, I stopped my professor after class and told him about a "friend" who wasn't tithing. I expected him to come back with quick judgment. Instead he said, "Study what the Bible says about where tithing originated. Note the difference between God's law covenant with Moses and Paul's grace teaching to the church. Then read Galatians. It tells us the law was bondage. Does your friend feel the bondage of guilt because he isn't following the law of tithing? Or is he resting in Christ, who has paid it all?"

While he did not give me the answer directly, I understood that he did not believe that tithing was for today. I almost asked, "Don't you think that my 'friend' is robbing God?" But I kept my mouth shut. What I learned that evening was there are two opposing opinions on this subject.

The principle of giving is taught in both the Old and New Testaments. The Israelites of the Old Testament and the Christians of the New Testament are called to be generous and open-handed with their finances. But how much does God want us to give?

Today, many are teaching that the members of Christ's body are still under the Old Testament obligation of giving a tenth of everything they earn, called a tithe, to the church. Others teach that we are no longer under this obligation and instead are under "grace giving," which means Christians give whatever the Lord leads them to give. Both sides believe they are interpreting the Bible correctly, and

INTRODUCTION

both views have very convincing arguments. So which is right?

Rather than accepting either teaching blindly, I decided to investigate what the Bible teaches on this subject.

After carefully studying the Scriptures, along with what others have to say about the subject, I am fully convinced we are not under an obligation to tithe. As a matter of fact, I would even take it a step further and say the Bible *commands* us not to teach tithing.

If you are consumed with shame and guilt for being unable to meet the radical demands of the tithe, I encourage you to read this booklet and learn how to give by the power and leading of the Holy Spirit, who speaks to our hearts rather than grudgingly or of necessity paying a mandatory tax.

> He who sows sparingly will also reap sparingly, and he who sows bountifully will also reap bountifully. So let each one give as he purposes in his heart, not grudgingly or of necessity; for God loves a cheerful giver.
> 2 Corinthians 9:6–7

I want to have the incredible Holy Spirit-led emotional experience of cheerfulness when I give. That is much more rewarding than meeting a forced financial obligation with an expectation of receiving earthly riches.

As I moved away from guilt and embraced Holy Spirit–led generosity, I became a better giver, within the church and outside of it. Over the years, I have met some incredibly generous Christians who are living by similar principles, and they have experienced incredible joy in their giving. Some are living in third-world countries and earn less than ten dollars a day, yet they still cheerfully give to the church and those in need. I also know people who have acquired great wealth and are giving millions of dollars by the leading of the Holy Spirit for the work of the gospel. They are not carefully calculating a percentage of their gross income. Instead, they have learned to hear the Holy Spirit and give as they purpose in their hearts, often giving greater amounts than 10 percent!

No matter what your economic position is today, you can experience great joy in the giving process. Come and explore what the Bible *truly* teaches us on how and what to contribute to the mission of the church, thus becoming a cheerful giver.

The *Cheerful* Giver

Spirit-Led Giving through New Testament Stewardship

CHAPTER ONE

Tithing

The word "tithe" means a tenth. The Hebrew word is *ma'aser*. It occurs thirty-two times in the Old Testament. The New Testament Greek equivalent is *dékato*. It is used four times: three times in the book of Hebrews and once in the book of Matthew.

I was twenty-one years old when I was invited to attend a Protestant church for the first time. During the service, when the time came for the collection of money, I wasn't prepared and I had only two quarters in my pocket. Panic filled me as the ushers made their way down the aisle with their large silver plates. The pastor prayed, "We give this money to You, Lord, as people obedient to Your will."

I opened one eye and saw him praying with his eyes wide open. I felt sure he was looking straight at me.

I contemplated my options. If I let the plate pass, everyone would stare at me and gasp. ("Marge, look at that disobedient person!") But if I dropped my two quarters in, everyone would hear them clink on the metal plate and judge me for being a cheapskate. Either way I'd be embarrassed.

The choir began to sing "Trust and Obey, there is no other way…" My face got hot and I felt sweat building on my forehead.

When the plate started down my row, I took out my wallet and pretended to pull out several bills. When it got to me, I swished my hand in the plate like I was mixing a bowl of salad. The lady next to me smiled at me, as if to say, "Good job, son." But I was thinking, *I'm going to hell.*

To be frank, I was confused and offended. I had no idea I had to pay to go to church!

That was thirty years ago. The collection of money at church no longer brings me anxiety. I now understand the idea of generously giving to the church. For believers, giving is an act of worship.

However, some Bible teachers and pastors claim this act of worship is mandatory. They say God requires all true believers to pay a tenth of everything they make to their local church.

Before we get to the subject of how much we should give, we must spend some time examining the principle of tithing. After all, this is where the controversy lies.

As the author of this book, I clearly believe the Bible is complete, inerrant, and infallible. I also believe the Bible is sufficient in its teaching for all matters related to the Christian faith. I say this because tithing teachers accuse non-tithers of having a weak and liberal theology. I would argue weak and liberal theology is anything contrary to what the Scriptures teach. As we move forward in this study, I will show that the weak and liberal theology actually belongs to the tithing teachers on this subject.

You may be asking me, "If you are so strong in Bible theology, why would you ignore all the Bible passages on tithing?" Let me be clear, I am not ignoring them. Remember, when I started this research task, I truly believed that tithing was for today. I had heard Bible teachers quote all the passages on tithing often and was convinced that is what the Bible teaches. But as I closely examined the context of these verses, I found these teachers are taking the tithing passages far out of context, allegorizing them, and wrongly applying them to today's local church. I do believe the Bible teaches *giving* as a modern-day church principle; however, *tithing* is not.

In this chapter, I will briefly go through all the Bible passages which teach tithing and show why they do not apply to us today. There are two primary arguments in favor of tithing: the Mosaic law argument and the patriarchal standard argument. Let's look at each one separately.

The Mosaic Law Argument in Favor of Tithing

With Moses, the Israelites had just crossed through the Red Sea and were filled with joy, but at the same time they were terrified. The only life they had ever known was slavery. Although unjust and cruel, at least they knew their Egyptian masters would provide food and a roof over their heads. But freedom far outweighed the risk, so they left Egypt, just as God through Moses had commanded. Now they were standing on the other side of the Red Sea, having witnessed Pharaoh's army being swept away by the waters. Over a million people stood there, hearts pounding, staring at the water and at the desert behind them. "We're free!"

Not so fast. Not long after the Israelites came out of Egypt, God gave them rules. *A lot of rules.* Six hundred and thirteen of them to be exact.

> There He [God] made a statute and an ordinance for them, and there He tested them, and said, "If you diligently heed the voice of the LORD your God and do what is right in His sight, give ear to His commandments and keep all His statutes, I will put none of the diseases on you which I have brought on the Egyptians. For I am the LORD who heals you."
>
> Exodus 15:25–26

"You're giving us rules?"

Yes. The first ten are what we call the Ten Commandments and another 603 followed. They are all contained in the books of Exodus, Leviticus, and Deuteronomy. Why rules? Because, without rules the Israelites would have gone their own way and turned to all kinds of evil. In addition, these rules were given so the Israelites could show and prove their devotion to God. Most important for the subject of this book, one of those 613 rules was the rule to tithe. The Lord said:

> All the tithe of the land, whether of the seed of the land or of the fruit of the tree, is the LORD's. It is

holy to the Lord. These are the commandments which the Lord commanded Moses for the children of Israel on Mount Sinai.
Leviticus 27:30, 34

Then God instructed the Israelites to give all of these tithes to the Levites for their purpose.

> Behold, I have given the children of Levi all the tithes in Israel as an inheritance in return for the work which they perform, the work of the tabernacle of meeting. Hereafter the children of Israel shall not come near the tabernacle of meeting, lest they bear sin and die. But the Levites shall perform the work of the tabernacle of meeting, and they shall bear their iniquity; it shall be a statute forever, throughout your generations, that among the children of Israel they shall have no inheritance. For the tithes of the children of Israel, which they offer up as a heave offering to the Lord, I have given to the Levites as an inheritance.
> Numbers 18:21-24

To understand why, we must remember eleven of the twelve tribes of Israel received land as their inheritance. Land requires work. *A lot of work.* The work consisted of raising livestock and planting crops so the people of each tribe could survive. However, the Levites did not receive land as an inheritance. Instead, they were appointed to be priests over Israel. Their purpose was to perform the work of the tabernacle where intercessions would be made for the sins of the Israelites. Therefore, the purpose of tithing was so the eleven tribes would support the tribe of Levi so they could devote full-time performance of the necessary priesthood duties, bearing the iniquity of *all* Israel.

Many preachers quote these Scripture passages and say today the local church is the modern equivalent of the Levitical priesthood and therefore members of the church are required to give 10 percent of their income to the church so pastors and church staff can perform the ministry of the gospel. However, there are problems with this reasoning.

First, the Mosaic law tithing teachers fail to teach *all of the tithes required by the law*. The law didn't just require one tithe of 10 percent. It actually required three separate tithes totaling 23.3 percent annually. I have already described the Levitical tithe above (Numbers 18:21-24) which is one nation supporting another. The second tithe was required of individuals and is called a tithe of feasts (Deuteronomy 14:22-27). This tithe was to be used in celebrating the annual feasts. Then a third tithe, also an individual requirement, was to be collected at the end of every third year and given to the "stranger and the fatherless and the widow who are within your gates" (Deuteronomy 14:28-29). This third tithe basically supported the poor who lived within the tribe. So there were actually three separate tithes required by the Mosaic law. To date, I have not met any Mosaic law tithers who teach we should give 23.3 percent of our income.

Second, we do not have a separate priesthood in the local church like the Israelites had. Following Christ's resurrection and the giving of the Holy Spirit, all believers are priests.

> But you are a chosen generation, a royal priesthood, a holy nation, His own special people, that you may proclaim the praises of Him who called you out of darkness into His marvelous light; who once were not a people but are now the people of God, who had not obtained mercy but now have obtained mercy.
> 1 Peter 2:9-10

This is a hallmark belief of the Protestant church: we are all priests of a holy nation, the universal church. There is no longer a separate Levitical priesthood or anything even close to it today. Yes, there are important tasks of the leaders of the local church; however, they do not make sacrifices nor do they bear the iniquity of their congregation. Today all believers have direct access to God. Amen?

Third, the New Testament says we are no longer under the Mosaic law:

> "For sin shall no longer be your master, because you are not under the law, but under grace."
> Romans 6:14 NIV

The New Testament gives a stern warning that not only are we no longer under the law, there is a danger for those who teach it.

> I marvel that you are turning away so soon from Him who called you in the grace of Christ, to a different gospel, which is not another; but there are some who trouble you and want to pervert the gospel of Christ. But even if we, or an angel from heaven, preach any other gospel to you than what we have preached to you, let him be accursed. As we have said before, so now I say again, if anyone preaches any other gospel to you than what you have received, let him be accursed.
>
> Galatians 1:6–9

This "different gospel, which is not another" is identified in the next chapter as the Mosaic law, and anyone teaching the Mosaic law as a requirement for today is accursed.

> For if I build again those things which I destroyed, I make myself a transgressor. For I through the law died to the law that I might live to God. I have been crucified with Christ; it is no longer I who live, but Christ lives in me; and the life which I now live in the flesh I live by faith in the Son of God, who loved me and gave Himself for me. I do not set aside the grace of God; for if righteousness comes through the law, then Christ died in vain."
>
> Galatians 2:18-21

The historical context of these verses is important to understand. The first century church was in a period of transition. Many Jews who had come to believe in Jesus were still trying to follow the Mosaic law. They were participating in festivals and Sabbaths, strictly following dietary regulations, performing religious circumcisions, and demanding that Gentile converts adhere to these laws too. The leadership of the church had to confront those who taught this and they concluded that those who preached the law were perverting the gospel of grace.

Some argue there is another verse in the New Testament which says the law *is* for today and will continue until the end of time. Jesus said:

> Do not think that I came to destroy the Law or the Prophets. I did not come to destroy but to fulfill. For assuredly, I say to you, till heaven and earth pass away, one jot or one tittle will by no means pass from the law till all is fulfilled. Whoever therefore breaks one of the least of these commandments, and teaches men so, shall be called least in the kingdom of heaven; but whoever does and teaches them, he shall be called great in the kingdom of heaven. For I say to you, that unless your righteousness exceeds the righteousness of the scribes and Pharisees, you will by no means enter the kingdom of heaven.
> Matthew 5:17–20

This appears to say that the law should be taught until "heaven and earth pass away." Is that a contradiction to Paul's teaching that the law has been abrogated? No. The law was and still is for those who are living under works (the unsaved). If we are obedient to one part of the law, then we need to be obedient to all of it (James 2:10). We already know it is impossible to live a perfect life, which is why we need Jesus's cross work and resurrection to free us from the bondage and consequences of breaking the law. Unfortunately, those who have not made the decision to follow Jesus are still under the law, and they will be judged by it.

> What purpose then does the law serve? It was added because of transgressions, till the Seed [Jesus] should come to whom the promise was made; and it was appointed through angels by the hand of a mediator. Now a mediator does not mediate for one only, but God is one. Is the law then against the promises of God? Certainly not! For if there had been a law given which could have given life, truly righteousness would have been by the law. But the Scripture has confined all under sin, that the promise by faith in Jesus Christ might be given to those who believe. But before faith came, we were kept under guard by the law, kept for the faith which would afterward be revealed. Therefore the law was our tutor to bring us to Christ, that we might be justified by faith. But after faith has come, we are no longer under a tutor [the law].
>
> Galatians 3:19–25

The law is bondage. Jesus fulfilled the law by dying for sin so there is no longer any condemnation or curse for those who believe. The price has been paid. Because of the work of Christ, we are now joined to Him by faith. He continually intercedes for us so we too are seen as righteous—not by any law works (such as tithing) but by His blood.

Logically the next question which is *often* raised is, "Since I am no longer under the law, which also says I should not murder, is it now okay for me to murder?" (Paul answers this in Romans 6:1–4)

> What shall we say then? Shall we continue in sin that grace may abound? Certainly not! How shall we who died to sin live any longer in it? Or do you not know that as many of us as were baptized into Christ Jesus were baptized into His death? Therefore we were buried with Him through baptism into death, that just as Christ was raised from the dead by the glory of the Father, even so we also should walk in newness of life.

Does "newness of life" mean we are following the Mosaic law? No. For those of us who believe and follow Jesus, the 613 Mosaic law commandments have been replaced by two.

> "Love the Lord your God with all your heart and with all your soul and with all your mind and with all your strength." The second is this: "Love your neighbor as yourself. There is no commandment greater than these."
>
> Mark 12:30-31 NIV

> For you, brethren, have been called to liberty; only do not use liberty as an opportunity for the flesh, but through love serve one another. For all the law is fulfilled in one word, even in this: "You shall love your neighbor as yourself."
>
> Galatians 5:13-14

The apostle Paul said evidence of the newness of life is as follows:

> I say then: Walk in the Spirit, and you shall not fulfill the lust of the flesh. For the flesh lusts against the Spirit, and the Spirit against the flesh; and these are contrary to one another, so that you do not do the things that you wish. But if you are led by the Spirit, you are not under the law. Now the works of the flesh are evident, which are: adultery, fornication, uncleanness, lewdness, idolatry, sorcery, hatred, contentions, jealousies, outbursts of wrath, selfish ambitions, dissensions, heresies, envy, murders, drunkenness, revelries, and the like; of which I tell you beforehand, just as I also told you in time past, that those who practice such things will not inherit the kingdom of God. But the fruit of the Spirit is love, joy, peace, longsuffering, kindness, goodness, faithfulness, gentleness, self-control. Against such there is no law. And those who are Christ's have crucified the flesh with its passions and desires. If we live in the Spirit, let us also walk in the Spirit. Let us not

become conceited, provoking one another, envying one another.

Galatians 5:16-26

The Patriarchal Standard in Favor of Tithing

Not all tithing teachers use the Mosaic Law as justification for their stance. Many of them would rightly agree we no longer observe the Mosaic law. Instead, they use an argument called the *patriarchal standard*, which says there was tithing before (or outside of) the Mosaic law. They show in Genesis that the patriarchs, Abram (Abraham) and Jacob who lived before Moses, both tithed: therefore, this proves God requires a tithe from all true believers for all of time.

Before I refute this argument, let's look at these two specific examples of the patriarchs tithing.

> After Abram returned from defeating Kedorlaomer and the kings allied with him, the king of Sodom came out to meet him in the Valley of Shaveh (that is, the King's Valley).
>
> Then Melchizedek king of Salem brought out bread and wine. He was priest of God Most High, and he blessed Abram, saying,
>
>> "Blessed be Abram by God Most High,
>> Creator of heaven and earth.
>> And blessed be to God Most High,
>> who delivered your enemies into your hand."

> Then Abram gave him a tenth of everything.
> Genesis 14:17–20 NIV

Abram gave the priest-king Melchizedek a tithe, 10 percent of *everything*. Then ten chapters later in the book of Genesis, Abraham's grandson Jacob awoke from his "ladder dream" where he had an encounter with God, and he made a vow that included a tithe:

> Jacob awoke from his sleep and said, "Surely the LORD is in this place, and I did not know it." And he was afraid and said, "How awesome is this place! This is none other than the house of God, and this is the gate of heaven!"... Then Jacob made a vow, saying, "If God will be with me, and keep me in this way that I am going, and give me bread to eat and clothing to put on, so that I come back to my father's house in peace, then the LORD shall be my God. And this stone which I have set as a pillar shall be God's house, and of all that You give me I will surely give a tenth to You."
> Genesis 28:16–22

Abram gave a tithe to Melchizedek; Jacob gave a tithe to God. Do these examples of the patriarchs tithing outside of the law prove that God initiated tithing for believers for all time? There are four ways to refute this argument:

First, there is no direct command from God that Abram was to give a tenth to Melchizedek, nor for Jacob to give directly to God. The Bible doesn't say why Abram and Jacob gave a tithe, they just did it. However, there is historical evidence that indicates it is probable Abram and Jacob were participating in a normal cultural practice of their day. Historians have documented the practice of tithing in the early Semitic time period. Many early Near East cultures and societies at the time of Abraham tithed to people who helped or ruled over them. The bottom line is God did not command it, nor does it say anywhere in the Bible that we are to transfer Abram and Jacob's examples of tithing to today.

Second, Abram's tithe to Melchizedek was not an ongoing act. He only gave a tenth to the king of Salem once. If we use Abram's tithe as an example for us today, then our tithing to the local church should only be a one-time event which no pro-tithers teach. Two of the four uses of the word *tithe* in the New Testament were referring to this event, which was not referring to the importance of the tithe, but the greatness of Melchizedek.

Third, Jacob would be a better example of ongoing tithing because the Bible implies Jacob gave a tithe to God indefinitely. However, Jacob's tithe was a vow made by Jacob, not required by God. We too can make vows to God. We may even vow to give 10 percent of our gross income to the local church, or we may vow to read the whole Bible in a year, or we may vow to give our lives to missionary work. There are millions of vows a believer can make to God. However, I would caution people to be careful when making vows. Vows, similar to covenants, are admirable but dangerous. If you miss even one day, then you break the whole vow. As we will learn later in this book, it is better (and safer) to live according to the direction of the Holy Spirit who knows our future and is able to direct us according to His will and our ability.

Fourth, the practice of circumcision was also a patriarchal practice which later became part of the Mosaic law. Abraham circumcised Isaac (Genesis 21:4). He did so because God commanded him to do it. However, the New Testament clearly teaches the practice of circumcision is not required today.

> Stand fast therefore in the liberty by which Christ has made us free, and do not be entangled again with a yoke of bondage. Indeed I, Paul, say to you that if you become circumcised, Christ will profit you nothing. And I testify again to every man who becomes circumcised that he is a debtor to keep the whole law. You have become estranged from Christ, you who attempt to be justified by law; you have fallen from grace. For we through the Spirit eagerly wait for the hope of righteousness by faith. For in Christ Jesus neither circumcision nor uncircumcision avails anything, but faith working through love.
>
> Galatians 5:1-6

If we no longer follow the Old Testament Abrahamic example of circumcision, why are people teaching we must follow the Abrahamic example of tithing?

All these reasons for not adhering to the Mosaic law nor the patriarchal standard of tithing comes from studying the context of the relative verses, plus the New Testament teaching on the Old Testament practices, and frankly just plain ole common sense. To say we need to follow the Old Testament examples of tithing as a rule for today requires quite a bit of Scripture twisting to fit a particular doctrine.

CHAPTER TWO

The Reward Passages on Tithing

Before we leave this subject and start exploring how to be a Holy Spirit-led, cheerful giver, we must address the reward passages which tithing teachers inevitably use to prompt people to give 10 percent of their income to their local church. Let's take a look at these passages. These too have been taken out of context.

As a new Christian, Cheryl wanted to learn everything she could about God. She joined an evangelical church where the pastor accurately taught from the Scriptures. She attended a women's Bible study and read her Bible every morning. One evening, while flipping through channels on her television, she came across a program where "evangelists" healed the sick. They said God promises great wealth and many blessings to those who follow and obey Him. This message struck Cheryl's heart. These people seemed to have far more faith than she did. As they called upon God to perform miracles, tumors vanished, epilepsy was cured, paralytics stood and walked. People in the audience cried and sang worship songs and praised God. It was beautiful!

The TV evangelist turned to the camera and said, "There is somebody at home watching this broadcast who's been out of work for several months. You don't know how you're going to pay your rent. God will provide if you trust Him."

A chill overcame Cheryl. She was out of work. Oh, how she wanted to trust God to help her!

At the end of the broadcast, the preacher asked for money to help continue the work of the ministry. He promised that those who sent money would receive health and wealth from God. He then quoted Malachi 3:8-10:

> "Will a man rob God?
> Yet you have robbed Me!
> But you say,
> 'In what way have we robbed You?'
> In tithes and offerings.
> You are cursed with a curse,
> For you have robbed Me,
> Even this whole nation.
> Bring all the tithes into the storehouse,
> That there may be food in My house,
> And try Me now in this,"
> Says the Lord of hosts,
> "If I will not open for you the windows of heaven
> And pour out for you such blessing
> That there will not be room enough to receive it."

THE REWARD PASSAGES ON TITHING

He read letters from people who'd given money to their ministry and were subsequently cured of cancer, or given a new car, or had their house mortgage paid off.

Cheryl pulled out her checkbook and sent them fifty of her last hundred dollars.

These are the "prosperity gospel" teachers who claim God promises health and wealth for all true followers of Jesus. However, they are really using the Word of God, and often fake miracles, to line their pockets with the money of people who are suffering and desperate. They drive around in luxury automobiles, live in lavish estates, and have hired servants who cook, clean, drive, and shop for them, while many of the people who follow them are desolate, giving their last dime for a small ray of hope.

This is a scam of the worst kind. Almost all of these "evangelists" use the concept of tithing with rewards to convince people to give their money regularly to their "ministry." However, today this teaching is not limited to "prosperity gospel" preachers. To a lesser extent, it has found its way into mainstream evangelical churches. The following is a quote from a book given to me by a tithing pastor which was written by an otherwise good teacher, who would never try to defraud people for personal gain. His audience is made up of people who just want to learn God's Word accurately, but his promise of rewards is very similar to the swindlers.

> Dream with me for a moment. Relax and imagine a reality in which you don't live without financial strain. You don't struggle to make ends meet each

month. You are completely out of debt. You aren't bound by the ties of materialism. Your needs are consistently met. You have the ability to save for your children's education or your retirement. You have the ability to help people in need. You have the ability to give to causes much bigger than your own concerns. You live life full of generosity, joy, and peace. The principles contained in this little book have the potential to turn these dreams into reality.³

Reading the book, we find the "principles contained in this little book" are the principles of tithing and rewards. The author says if we tithe, all of our financial needs will be met and more.

In the introduction of this book, I gave another example of a well-known finance seminar which has been attended by millions of Christians worldwide, which also teaches tithing with rewards. Unlike the prosperity gospel preachers, I don't think these teachers are purposely trying to defraud their hearers. Often, they are just following tradition and teaching which has not been fully vetted.

One such pastor once told me, "John, I know what you are saying and I believe it. However, I am a third-generation pastor in the same church where my father and grandfather ministered. I have people in my congregation who have tithed seventy-plus years based on their teaching. They would all string me up if I taught anything other than the tithe."

---

3   Searcy, Nelson. *The Generosity Ladder.* (Grand Rapids: Baker Books, 2010) Pages 7-8

THE REWARD PASSAGES ON TITHING

I get that. Traditions and history are very important. However, in Matthew 14, Jesus clearly teaches the Word of God transcends the tradition of men.

Back to Malachi 3:8-10.

> "Will a man rob God?
> Yet you have robbed Me!
> But you say,
> 'In what way have we robbed You?'
> In tithes and offerings.
> You are cursed with a curse,
> For you have robbed Me,
> Even this whole nation.
> Bring all the tithes into the storehouse,
> That there may be food in My house,
> And try Me now in this,"
> Says the Lord of hosts,
> "If I will not open for you the windows of heaven
> And pour out for you such blessing
> That there will not be room enough to receive it."

At first glance these verses do seem to imply that God will bless us with riches beyond our imagination when we tithe. There are several reasons why we shouldn't use this passage as an example to tithe.

First of all, the Malachi passage was not referring to money. When we look at the context of this passage, we see that it is really referring to animal sacrifices. After the Israelites came back from exile in the sixth century BC, they rebuilt the temple that was destroyed by the Babylonians.

We learn they failed to follow the Mosaic law regarding animal sacrifices. Instead of using animals without blemish, they used animals which were "defiled," "blind," "lame," and "sick," as well as "contemptible fruit and food" as their offerings (Malachi 1:12).

The Lord was displeased by these offerings, and He told them to stop. He said, "Bring your best to the table to proclaim to all the nations that God is great and worthy of the best. Stop holding back on your tithes that are needed to support the Levites and priests so they can do the work of the Lord."

This passage was never intended to be an example of monetary sacrifice for all time. The sacrificial system has been done away with when Jesus died on the cross, when He bore the sins of the world. Those who teach this verse as a necessity for money tithing with the promise of material and health rewards are perverting the gospel of grace and abrogating Christ's body and blood payment.

Second, under the Mosaic law, the Israelites lived with a system of blessings and curses. If Israel followed God by obeying His commandments, they would be blessed. If they turned from God and followed idols, they would endure curses (Deuteronomy 28).

Today, we no longer live under the law which promises blessings and curses. The New Testament says that today when we follow God we will be persecuted by enduring trials and suffering for His sake. Sounds a lot like curses, right? But suffering today is not a curse. As followers of Jesus Christ, being poor can be a blessing; getting sick can be a blessing; being imprisoned for the gospel or even martyred for your faith can be a blessing.

Second Corinthians 1:3–6 says:

> Blessed be the God and Father of our Lord Jesus Christ, the Father of mercies and God of all comfort, who comforts us in all our tribulation, that we may be able to comfort those who are in any trouble, with the comfort with which we ourselves are comforted by God. For as the sufferings of Christ abound in us, so our consolation also abounds through Christ. Now if we are afflicted, it is for your consolation and salvation, which is effective for enduring the same sufferings which we also suffer. Or if we are comforted, it is for your consolation and salvation.

We are witnesses of the gospel through our suffering. You cannot avoid suffering by giving more money.

Second Corinthians 12:9–10 says there is power in weakness:

> He said to me, "My grace is sufficient for you, for My strength is made perfect in weakness." Therefore most gladly I will rather boast in my infirmities, that the power of Christ may rest upon me. Therefore I take pleasure in infirmities, in reproaches, in needs, in persecutions, in distresses, for Christ's sake. For when I am weak, then I am strong.

In the midst of our suffering, we can rest assured that "all things work together for good to those who love God, to those who are the called according to His purpose" (Romans 8:28).

We cannot interpret suffering as a punishment or wealth as a blessing. Yes, suffering may be a way for God to correct us. Or it may just be a consequence of living in a sin-cursed world. Or perhaps it is a means for God to proclaim His greatness.

From man's perspective this sounds foolish. Wouldn't it be better for God to make all Christians successful and disease free as soon as they come to faith? Health and wealth are much better advertisements for the gospel than persecution and suffering?

First Corinthians 1:26–27 says:

> For you see your calling, brethren, that not many wise according to the flesh, not many mighty, not many noble, are called. But God has chosen the foolish things of the world to put to shame the wise, and God has chosen the weak things of the world to put to shame the things which are mighty;

Prosperity gospel preachers tell people that when they tithe, they will receive a comfort blessing in the form of living without financial strain or not struggling to make ends meet or being able to save for their children's education and their own retirement. This is a lie. Our hope is not in this present world. People who give tithes today still die; they still suffer; they still experience poverty.

THE REWARD PASSAGES ON TITHING

The Scriptures actually say that wealth can be a barrier to faith and belief. Jesus said in Mark 10:25, "It is easier for a camel to go through the eye of a needle than for a rich man to enter the kingdom of God." Why would God reward His people with an object that can be a barrier to faith?

First Timothy 6:6–1 says:

> Now godliness with contentment is great gain. For we brought nothing into this world, and it is certain we can carry nothing out. And having food and clothing, with these we shall be content. But those who desire to be rich fall into temptation and a snare, and into many foolish and harmful lusts which drown men in destruction and perdition. For the love of money is a root of all kinds of evil, for which some have strayed from the faith in their greediness, and pierced themselves through with many sorrows.

It takes a strong and faithful person to handle wealth God's way. I know some wealthy men and women who give generously, witness to their neighbors, support the church, and live humbly. But I have also seen Christians receive great wealth then fall in love with their money, and their worldly lusts overcome their desire, passion, and need for the Lord.

Wealth isn't bad in and of itself. But we cannot interpret wealth as a blessing.

The pro-tithing folks can cite examples of people who gave a tithe and soon after received money, a promotion, or some other blessing. However, if only one person did not receive a blessing after giving a full tithe, their theory would be disproved. And there are many.

My friend Tom was convinced he needed to tithe. At church one Sunday, to his wife's horror, he wrote a check for $1,200 and dropped it into the offering plate. He was very excited about his "obedience" and shared this testimony with his friends. Two weeks later, he was laid off from his job, which caused a great financial hardship for his family, and a tremendous crisis of faith for Tom.

The response of the pro-tithing group is that those who give financially may receive blessings in other ways.

> Do not worry, saying, "What shall we eat?" or "What shall we drink?" or "What shall we wear?" For after all these things the Gentiles seek. For your heavenly Father knows that you need all these things. *But give 10 percent of your net income after deductions for capital expenditures to your local church, and all these things shall be added to you.*
>
> Matthew 6:31–33

No, wait. Verse 33 doesn't say that. It actually says: "But seek first the kingdom of God and His righteousness, and all these things shall be added to you."

It isn't tithing that creates the miracle of God's provision; it's the love of God, who continually provides for His people. God meets our needs not because we tithe but because He loves us.

Check out verses 25–30:

THE REWARD PASSAGES ON TITHING

> Do not worry about your life, what you will eat or what you will drink; nor about your body, what you will put on. Is not life more than food and the body more than clothing? Look at the birds of the air, for they neither sow nor reap nor gather into barns; yet your heavenly Father feeds them. Are you not of more value than they? Which of you by worrying can add one cubit to his stature? So why do you worry about clothing? Consider the lilies of the field, how they grow: they neither toil nor spin; and yet I say to you that even Solomon in all his glory was not arrayed like one of these. Now if God so clothes the grass of the field, which today is, and tomorrow is thrown into the oven, will He not much more clothe you, O you of little faith?

We should never give because we expect something in return. Here is another passage often quoted by prosperity tithers:

> Give, and it will be given to you: good measure, pressed down, shaken together, and running over will be put into your bosom. For with the same measure that you use, it will be measured back to you.
> Luke 6:38

Tithing teachers say, "Hey. Here you go. This is a New Testament passage which teaches tithing" Although it is similar to Malachi 3, this passage has a different context and is not referring to tithing or anything close to it. The context of this passage is this: starting in Luke 6:27, the gospel writer is talking about how to love our enemies. It is about serving those who are against us. In other words, it says when we love our enemies, God will do amazing things!

All of these passages used by the tithing teachers are based on works. They are part of the covenant that said, "If you do this, God will do that." However, today we are under a new covenant by the blood of Jesus (Matthew 26:28), and it is *unconditional*. Being saved apart from works distinguishes Christianity from all other religions. Let's not go back to the law, which was bondage to the Israelites. We are free in Christ! Amen.

CHAPTER THREE

Woo Hoo! It's All Mine!

N ow, let's look at what Scripture says about managing our possessions, how and when to give, and how to experience great joy (cheerfulness) in doing so.

First, let's look at stewardship, which provides the foundation for the biblical way to give. Paul uses this term in Ephesians 3:1–2:

> For this reason I, Paul, the prisoner of Christ Jesus for you Gentiles—if indeed you have heard of the *stewardship* of the grace of God which was given to me for you (NASB; emphasis added).

Peter also uses the term in 1 Peter 4:10:

> As each one has received a gift, minister it to one another, as good *stewards* of the manifold grace of God (emphasis added).

"Stewardship" in Greek is *oikonomia,* meaning "the management of a household or of household affairs." The first part, *oikos,* means "a house," and *nomos* means "a law."[4] Merriam-Webster's dictionary defines a steward as "a person whose job is to manage the land and property of another person."[5]

A steward is a servant. We are servants of God, and the money we possess really belongs to Him. We are the stewards of God's money.

Alicia, a friend of mine who is a devout Christian, told me this story:

> I was a bookkeeper for a doctor. I created his budget, kept his books, paid his bills, and did anything else he needed me to do. He trusted me with everything, so much so that he never checked to see if I was doing anything dishonest.
>
> One day, my husband lost his job. We quickly started going into debt. When an opportunity came along to take a little money from the business, I made a check out to myself and slipped it into the big pile of checks my boss signed each morning. It wasn't unusual for a check to be addressed to me, because I sometimes made cash transactions for him.
>
> I justified this by thinking, *The business has so much money nobody will ever notice. Besides, I've*

---

4   *Vine's Complete Expository Dictionary of Old and New Testament Words* (Nashville: Thomas Nelson Publishers, 1996)

5   http://www.merriam-webster.com/dictionary/steward.

WOO HOO! IT'S ALL MINE!

done a lot of work for the company on my own time that I was never reimbursed for, so frankly, I deserve it.

I stood there while he signed the checks. He didn't blink an eye when mine came up. It was so easy I started sliding more checks into the pile. I promised myself I'd stop once my husband and I got caught up with our bills. But something else happened that put us further in debt. Something else *always* happened. So I kept taking more money.

I even became self-righteous with it. I gave money to other people in need. It boosted my self-esteem, because I became the person everyone went to when they were having financial troubles.

After a while, guilt caught up with me. I started having panic attacks. I became seriously depressed. I knew the Holy Spirit was hounding me. So I stopped stealing from my boss. But the depression continued.

Eventually, I concluded that I needed to tell my boss everything. It took every ounce of courage within me to walk into his office that day. Seeing me crying and shaking, he asked what was wrong. I told him what I had done.

He was silent for a while. Disappointment etched his face. He thanked me for being honest, and he told me if I paid him back, he would not report me. I assured him I would go through all the books and repay every dime I had taken. That was one of the most freeing things I have ever done.

But when his wife found out, she called the police. After a long court battle, I ended up spending two years in a federal prison. And I deserved it. I was wrong.

Alicia is an amazing woman who learned a difficult and valuable lesson about the consequences of being a bad steward of someone else's money. She now speaks to women's groups, telling them about her story of repentance and redemption.

If she had remained silent, nobody would have found out about her crime. But she listened to the Holy Spirit, did the right thing, and paid the price. And now she is restored.

I have a confession to make. I too am guilty of being a bad steward of someone else's money. God's. Which is why I ended up in a financial seminar in the first place; hoping for a solution to get out of overwhelming debt which was created by buying a lot of things I could have done without or at least waited until I could afford them.

As Christians we are called to manage God's money well. But what does this mean? Does this mean we cannot buy a nice car, or go on an expensive vacation, or splurge on decorations for our home? No. Having and doing nice things is not a sin. However, if we are greedy with all of it then we are missing out on a great opportunity. We may be comfortable in this life, but paupers in the next.

> Do not store up for yourselves treasures on earth, where moth and rust destroy, and where thieves

break in and steal. But store up for yourselves treasures in heaven, where moth and rust do not destroy, and where thieves do not break in and steal. For where your treasure is, there your heart will be also.

Matthew 6:19-21 NIV

"Everyone to whom much is given, from him much will be required." (Luke 12:48) Those of us who can afford to must be generous with our money and possessions.

The new covenant command for Christian giving is in 2 Corinthians 9:6–8:

> He who sows sparingly will also reap sparingly, and he who sows bountifully will also reap bountifully. So let each one give as he purposes in his heart, not grudgingly or of necessity; for God loves a cheerful giver. And God is able to make all grace abound toward you, that you, always having all sufficiency in all things, may have an abundance for every good work.

Verse 8 sounds like the prosperity gospel. However, this passage is not teaching us that when we give money, we will receive a financial reward to live more comfortably. It says when we give, God will provide more "for every good work." When we are faithful with little, He will entrust us with more for His ministry, not for our pleasure. "Reaping bountifully" as a steward is reaping bountifully for the Master, not ourselves. Let me say it again, *reaping bountifully as a steward is reaping bountifully for the Master, not ourselves.* This is the key difference between us and the tithing teachers.

Also, Paul makes it clear that giving is not a commandment. We do it out of love for one another.

> I speak not by commandment, but I am testing the sincerity of your love by the diligence of others.
>
> 2 Corinthians 8:8

There is no commandment or law to give. We are to love through the working of the Holy Spirit, which means one month God may lead you to give a dollar to your local church. The next month, He may inspire you to give thousands of dollars to a charitable organization. He may even draw you to give millions! If you listen to the Holy Spirit, you'll know what God wants you to do.

Tithing a set amount diminishes the role of the Holy Spirit to direct our giving decisions. Instead, it makes tithing similar to a tax debt. And who enjoys paying those?

How does the Holy Spirit lead us to manage God's money properly? Two ways.

First, and it is related to the title of this book. The original Greek words for cheerful is *hilaros*. As tithing teachers rightfully point out, this is where we get our English word hilarious. However, *hilaros* does not mean crazy. It signifies the readiness of mind, that joyousness, which is prompt to do anything; hence, "cheerful." In the Septuagint (the Greek translation of the Old Testament which Jesus used) is the verb *hilaruno* which translates a Hebrew word meaning "to cause to shine" (Psalm 104:15)[6]. In other words, when we have "readiness of mind" the Holy Spirit "prompts" us to give and therefore, "causes us to shine." In other words, the Holy Spirit gives us pleasure when we heed His voice. None of that happens when we do it out of necessity. In the next chapter, I will be talking more about how to hear the Holy Spirit on these matters.

The second way the Holy Spirit leads us to manage God's money properly is *love*. Consider this scene from Luke 10:25–37:

> A certain lawyer stood up and tested [Jesus], saying, "Teacher, what shall I do to inherit eternal life?"
>
> He said to him, "What is written in the law? What is your reading of it?"
>
> So he answered and said, "'You shall love the Lord your God with all your heart, with all your soul, with all your strength, and with all your mind,' and 'your neighbor as yourself.'"
>
> And He said to him, "You have answered rightly; do this and you will live."
>
> But he, wanting to justify himself, said to Jesus, "And who is my neighbor?"
>
> Then Jesus answered and said: "A certain man went down from Jerusalem to Jericho, and fell among thieves, who stripped him of his clothing, wounded him, and departed, leaving him half

---

6   *Vine's Complete Expository Dictionary of Old and New Testament Words* (Nashville: Thomas Nelson Publishers, 1996)

dead. Now by chance a certain priest came down that road. And when he saw him, he passed by on the other side. Likewise a Levite, when he arrived at the place, came and looked, and passed by on the other side. But a certain Samaritan, as he journeyed, came where he was. And when he saw him, he had compassion. So he went to him and bandaged his wounds, pouring on oil and wine; and he set him on his own animal, brought him to an inn, and took care of him. On the next day, when he departed, he took out two denarii, gave them to the innkeeper, and said to him, 'Take care of him; and whatever more you spend, when I come again, I will repay you.' So which of these three do you think was neighbor to him who fell among the thieves?"

And he said, "He who showed mercy on him."

Then Jesus said to him, "Go and do likewise."

How do we love our neighbor as Jesus instructed? By giving to anyone who has need. What motivates us to give? Love. Where do we get that love? Only by supernatural means through the powerful work of the Holy Spirit.

A church I once attended had a food and clothes drive for the poor in our area. The pastor challenged the congregation to raise money and bring in nonperishable food and new or gently used clothes. They raised eight thousand dollars in cash and collected four tons of food and clothing in less than a week.

In the worship service that followed, we rejoiced! We laughed! We had great joy! We were cheerful! Because God had accomplished something only He could do.

What if instead the pastor had said, "Next week everyone in the church is required to give ten percent of their paychecks for the poor"? I'm not sure anyone would have done it, except those who have a lot of money or a lot of guilt.

Even if tithing brings in more money for church ministry, we must teach the biblical way of giving, not the traditions of men. The results are up to God.

To unbelievers, giving cheerfully may seem crazy. Why would anybody give up their hard-earned dollars to the church? Or even more puzzling, why would we give to strangers, some of whom don't appear to want to help themselves? While the world establishes social programs which help those who are well off to feel less guilty, the Holy Spirit moves us to love others as a natural byproduct of God's love for us. How hilarious is that!

CHAPTER FOUR

Cheerful Stewards of God's Money

Okay, so I hope I have made a good case against the practice of mandatory tithing and replaced it with stewardship and Holy Spirit-led giving. A pastor once said, "Instead of asking God how much we should give, we should be asking Him how much He wants us to keep!" Okay, so we ask. Now what? How do we hear God's response? Here are twelve ways the Bible says we hear God and how to be good stewards of God's money. Note: this is not law. This is for people who want to have a better relationship with God and hear His voice. Think of it more like a counseling session. Relational counseling. And the Bible is our counselor.

1. **Good stewards give not because of law but because they love the Father.**

In the last chapter we went in-depth about stewardship. However, whenever we hear the word *steward* we often think of butlers, maids, and cooks. Old movies typically portray stewards as being quiet, reserved, and obedient. ("Yes, ma'am." "Right away, sir.") These servants have a distant, professional relationship with the master. They sometimes serve out of fear. Do something wrong and you could find yourself looking for another job.

This is not the biblical concept of stewardship. Yes, we are God's servants, but we are also sons and daughters of the Master, joint heirs with Christ. He's not going to fire us for leaving spots on the silverware.

God has made us part of His family. Being part of a family means we have certain responsibilities. Chores, so to speak. My wife and I provide for the needs of our children, but we also assign them chores—not out of duty, but because we love them. They do their chores because they love us. It's all part of the family love dynamic. As children of God, we want to please our Father because we love Him. We develop a familial relationship with Him through worship, Bible study, prayer, and serving.

One of the ways we love and serve our Father is sharing our money and possessions with others. This is not easy to do. This ability to share only comes from the Father. It is a love action.

> Beloved, let us love one another, for love is of God; and everyone who loves is born of God and knows God. He who does not love does not know God, for God is love.
>
> 1 John 4:7-8

This love initiated by God gives us deep compassion for people in need, and as good stewards we willingly give. Do you have joy when you share? I know you do because I do. I was selfish before coming to know the Lord. Now I get an energy boost when giving. Sometimes I even "whoop!" You and I whoop because we fulfill a love opportunity and it feels great! That cheerful feeling comes from the Holy Spirit and it confirms that it is right to give.

2. Good stewards listen and obey.

We can't obey if we don't know what He wants us to do. How does an invisible God talk to us? Listening to God is a much larger subject than this book can address; however, I'd like to touch on two important aspects of it.

First, the Bible is the ultimate voice of God.

> All Scripture is given by inspiration of God, and is profitable for doctrine, for reproof, for correction, for instruction in righteousness, that the man of God may be complete, thoroughly equipped for every good work.
> 2 Timothy 3:16-17

So, if we want to hear God, we must first read the Scriptures. Every thought, feeling, and circumstance must be tested against the truth found within those sacred pages. It is the "living word" of God:

> The word of God is *living* and powerful, and sharper than any two-edged sword, piercing even to the division of soul and spirit, and of joints and marrow, and is a discerner of the thoughts and intents of the heart.
>
> Hebrews 4:12 (emphasis added)

When trying to hear and decipher God's will for our lives, we must immerse ourselves in the Word of God daily. Don't bother looking for a visible sign from God if you're ignoring Scripture. Personal experience alone does not constitute divine guidelines for living a godly life.

Second, to hear God's voice, we must be in tune with the Spirit rather than the flesh. Romans 8:5–6 says:

> Those who live according to the flesh set their minds on the things of the flesh, but those who live according to the Spirit, the things of the Spirit. For to be carnally minded is death, but to be spiritually minded is life and peace.

When we are living in sin, God's ears are closed to our prayers. First Peter 3:12 says, "The eyes of the Lord are on the righteous, and His ears are open to their prayers; but the face of the Lord is against those who do evil."

The voice of the Spirit and the voice of the flesh sound very similar so it is hard to differentiate between the two. In order for us to make sure we are hearing the Spirit rather than the flesh we must live holy lives. We need to mature in our faith by putting away evil things, then the voice of the

Spirit of God becomes so much clearer. When we are living holy lives and regularly reading and studying the Word of God, the Holy Spirit will guide us through circumstances and inner wisdom. We will know in our hearts what is best (2 Corinthians 9:7).

After hearing we must obey. *Obedience,* like *stewardship* can also be an awkward word. Because we live in an individualistic, self-reliant culture, obedience is difficult. Obedience is associated with reward or punishment. God's version of obedience is not much different. Obey God and you will receive reward. However, the reward is not being rich and illness free. Our reward is joy, assurance of salvation, and secure parental attachment knowing our heavenly Father loves us.

So what happens when we hear God's instruction and we don't obey? Just as there are many verses in the Bible which says we are to obey God, there are also many verses which says we are to fear God. The reason for this is when we ignore the Holy Spirit, we could end up being disciplined (chastened). However, our discipline is different than a strict boss who will easily fire us, never to see us again. As God's children He often chastises us with the goal of teaching us His will for our lives.

> "My son, do not despise the chastening of the Lord,
> Nor be discouraged when you are rebuked by Him;
> For whom the Lord loves He chastens,
> And scourges every son whom He receives."

> If you endure chastening, God deals with you as with sons; for what son is there whom a father does not chasten? But if you are without chastening, of which all have become partakers, then you are illegitimate and not sons. Furthermore, we have had human fathers who corrected *us,* and we paid them respect. Shall we not much more readily be in subjection to the Father of spirits and live? For they indeed for a few days chastened us as seemed best to them, but He for our profit, that we may be partakers of His holiness. Now no chastening seems to be joyful for the present, but painful; nevertheless, afterward it yields the peaceable fruit of righteousness to those who have been trained by it.
>
> Hebrews 12:5-7

When I was in fifth grade, my friend and I figured out how to make fake coins that would be accepted in vending machines. It was like becoming rich. We went to the arcade and played video games for hours. We bought an unlimited supply of candy bars. Then one day, after playing baseball at the park, we told everyone we would get sodas for them. We then went to the gas station and bought twelve sodas from the outside vending machine. Word spread that David and Johnny were giving away free sodas and soon every kid in the neighborhood wanted a free soda. We became the most popular kids around. But the gas station owner became suspicious and nabbed us during one of our heists. He knew my dad and it took many months of recycling newspapers to pay him back. I look back today and I am so thankful I was caught. It brought me back to being a law-abiding citizen. God disciplines us not out of revenge, but because He wants to restore us and make us better people. We shouldn't worry when He disciplines us, we should worry when He doesn't.

When it comes to money and how much God wants us to give, and really every area of our spiritual life, we need to immerse ourselves in the Scriptures, ask Him for wisdom, maintain a holy life, accept discipline when we do not, then listen and obey His voice.

3. Good stewards are precise with their finances and manage them wisely.

I hate managing my finances. It takes a lot of work. It's much easier just to buy whatever I want and then hope I've got money left in the bank account at the end of the month. But this never works. In the introduction of this book I mentioned a twelve-week finance seminar. Other than the teaching of the tithe, I would wholly support this ministry. My wife and I still use most of the principles taught in this seminar and are living a debt-free life, which allows us to give much more than when we were living a guilt-led life.

As faithful stewards of God's money, one of the most important things we can do is create a budget for our spending. If you don't know how to do this, find a book on the subject. Some churches offer financial seminars that can be highly beneficial as well.

Deciding where and how to spend your money requires a lot of wisdom. The book of Proverbs contains many verses about budgeting, debt, lending, giving, and greed. Here are a few:

> The plans of the diligent lead surely to plenty, but those of everyone who is hasty, surely to poverty.
> Proverbs 21:5

> He who has a slack hand becomes poor, but the hand of the diligent makes rich.
> Proverbs 10:4

> He who gathers in summer is a wise son; he who sleeps in harvest is a son who causes shame.
> Proverbs 10:5

God wants His people to act wisely and with common sense in every area of our lives, including what we do with our money. How do we develop wisdom? The Bible says we can ask God for it.

> If any of you lacks wisdom, let him ask of God, who gives to all liberally and without reproach, and it will be given to him. But let him ask in faith, with no doubting, for he who doubts is like a wave of the sea driven and tossed by the wind. For let not that man suppose that he will receive anything from the Lord; he is a double-minded man, unstable in all his ways.
> James 1:5–6

4. Stewards hold on to their possessions with open hands, not closed fists.

> Now behold, one said to Him, "Good Teacher, what good thing shall I do that I may have eternal life?" He replied, "Why do you call Me good? No one is good but One, that is, God. But if you want to enter into life, keep the commandments."
>
> He said to Him, "Which ones?"
>
> Jesus said, "'You shall not murder,' 'You shall not commit adultery,' 'You shall not steal,' 'You shall not bear false witness,' 'Honor your father and your mother,' and, 'You shall love your neighbor as yourself.'"
>
> The young man said to Him, "All these things I have kept from my youth. What do I still lack?"
>
> Jesus said to him, "If you want to be perfect, go, sell what you have and give to the poor, and you will have treasure in heaven; and come, follow Me."
>
> But when the young man heard that saying, he went away sorrowful, for he had great possessions.
>
> Matthew 19:16–22

What possession do you have that you cannot live without? If you lost everything in a house fire, what would you be most distraught over? What do you have that you would never let someone borrow? Is there anything so valuable that you would be willing to lose your life, or a friendship, or someone else's life in order to keep?

I have a collection of baseball cards in a shoebox. I've had it since the late 1960s. My mother bought most of these cards for me, one pack at a time, so they hold a lot of sentimental value. Some are worth a lot of money. Even though they're just collecting dust in my closet, I would have a hard time letting them go.

My friends in Mexico have the opposite attitude toward possessions, so I have to be careful what I say to them. If I said, "That's a beautiful picture on your wall," they would immediately take it off the wall, hand it to me, and say, "Here, it is yours." And if I didn't take it, they would be offended. For them, friendships mean more than possessions.

Loving anything so much that we would not part with it under any circumstances makes that possession an idol. That is called having closed fists; holding on to your possessions tightly. Closed fists not only are unable to give, they are also unable to receive. Open hands allow God to take and give freely. Has God ever taken something away from you, only to give you something better in its place?

5. Good stewards don't store up possessions.
Matthew 6:19–21 says:

> Do not lay up for yourselves treasures on earth, where moth and rust destroy and where thieves break in and steal; but lay up for yourselves treasures in heaven, where neither moth nor rust destroys and where thieves do not break in and steal. For where your treasure is, there your heart will be also.

Jesus had a warning for people who spend all their time increasing wealth and storing up earthly treasures. "Beware, and be on your guard against every form of greed; for not even when one has an abundance does his life consist of his possessions" (Luke 12:15 NASB). Then He told them a parable.

> The land of a rich man was very productive. And he began reasoning to himself, saying, "What shall I do, since I have no place to store my crops?" Then he said, "This is what I will do: I will tear down my barns and build larger ones, and there I will store all my grain and my goods. And I will say to my soul, 'Soul, you have many goods laid up for many years to come; take your ease, eat, drink and be merry.'
> But God said to him, "You fool! This very night your soul is required of you; and now who will own what you have prepared?"
> So is the man who stores up treasure for himself, and is not rich toward God.
> Luke 12:16–21 NASB

It is not wrong to be rich or to have valuable possessions. One of Jesus's disciples, Joseph of Arimathea, was rich. His property ownership played an important part in the burial and resurrection of Jesus.

> Now when evening had come, there came a rich man from Arimathea, named Joseph, who himself

> had also become a disciple of Jesus. This man went to Pilate and asked for the body of Jesus. Then Pilate commanded the body to be given to him. And when Joseph had taken the body, he wrapped it in a clean linen cloth, and laid it in his new tomb which he had hewn out of the rock; and he rolled a large stone against the door of the tomb, and departed.
>
> Matthew 27:57–60

If you can afford it, go ahead and buy that new car, remodel your kitchen, go on that fabulous vacation, surprise your wife with a nice piece of jewelry. But ask yourself, *What is the purpose for this purchase?* Are you using it merely for pleasure, or is there a larger purpose?

Ecclesiastes tells us the pleasures of this world have no meaning. They are all vanity and self-worship. Christians are called to a higher purpose: self-denial.

> Jesus said to His disciples, "If anyone desires to come after Me, let him deny himself, and take up his cross, and follow Me. For whoever desires to save his life will lose it, but whoever loses his life for My sake will find it. For what profit is it to a man if he gains the whole world, and loses his own soul? Or what will a man give in exchange for his soul? For the Son of Man will come in the glory of His Father with His angels, and then He will reward each according to his works.
>
> Matthew 16:24–27

Having possessions is not bad; however, when our possessions become our obsession, when they become something we cannot live without, or when we do not use them for the work of Christ, we are fools.

6. Good stewards give to their local church.

Some people worry that if a congregation isn't taught to tithe, the church will not have enough monetary support to continue. This attitude reveals a lack of faith that God will provide for the needs of the church without strong-arming its members with laws.

If the church's needs are not being met by the members, there may be a breakdown in communication between the leadership and the congregation. Or perhaps the members haven't been taught to listen to the Holy Spirit's guidance. Or maybe God might want the church to downsize its budget.

Just because there is no biblical requirement for us to tithe, that doesn't mean we shouldn't give to the church. The church is our family. In the context of a local assembly, we meet fellow believers and love one another. That is what the first church did.

> Now all who believed were together, and had all things in common, and sold their possessions and goods, and divided them among all, as anyone had need. So continuing daily with one accord in the temple, and breaking bread from house to house, they ate their food with gladness and simplicity of

> heart, praising God and having favor with all the people. And the Lord added to the church daily those who were being saved.
>
> Acts 2:44–47

While the makeup of the church has changed since the time of the early church, its purpose hasn't. Loving God and loving one another is still our main focus. Our job is to be the hands and feet of the gospel.

> You shall receive power when the Holy Spirit has come upon you; and you shall be witnesses to Me in Jerusalem, and in all Judea and Samaria, and to the end of the earth.
>
> Acts 1:8

Our desire should be to reach as many people with the gospel as possible. One pastor said the job of the church is to bring people in, build them up, and send them out. But all these things cost money.

The question comes down to *How much should we give to the church?* It is easier to have a specific number, like 10 percent, than to try to figure it out on an individual basis.

Making this decision requires us to spend focused time praying and discerning the Holy Spirit's leading. That can seem like too much work. We may be tempted to throw our hands up and say, "Forget it. Here's your ten percent!" But the work isn't burdensome if you look at it as a time of fellowship with God, worshiping, speaking our requests, and listening to our Father.

Don't trade your special time with God for a law. Wouldn't you rather hear directly from God?

When you do hear, obey. Give abundantly, if you are able to, and you will experience great joy!

> Concerning the collection for the saints, as I have given orders to the churches of Galatia, so you must do also: On the first day of the week let each one of you lay something aside, storing up as he may prosper, that there be no collections when I come.
>
> 1 Corinthians 16:1–2

The early church was collecting for "the saints." Although we are all called saints, the individuals referred to in this passage were the full-time ministers who relied on donations for their livelihood.

It is important to support our full-time ministers today. Paul said to his followers, "If we have sown spiritual things for you, is it a great thing if we reap your material things? If others are partakers of this right over you, are we not even more?" (1 Corinthians 9:11).

If a congregation is financially able, they should pay their pastors from donations.

It takes a lot of money to run a church today. Salaries, buildings, maintenance, utilities, missionaries, adult and children's ministries, and a hundred other expenditures add up quickly. But when we give money to the local church, in love, we get to participate in the "reaping" of souls for the sake of Christ (2 Corinthians 9:6). This is true grace giving.

7. Good stewards give outside of the church.

There are many ministries besides the church that need financial help to fulfill their purposes. Missionaries, hospitals, prisons, world hunger relief, disaster assistance, and church planting are all worthy recipients. According to the National Center for Charitable Statistics there are 1.56 million non-profit/charitable organizations in the United States alone.[7]

A tither may be tempted to say, "I give my full ten percent at the church. I am not required to give anything else." If your giving is directed by the prompting of the Holy Spirit, you will be able to discern whether God has chosen you to participate in being a blessing to individuals or organizations beyond the needs of your local church.

Perhaps your neighbor is having a hard time making ends meet, and your gift would be an answer to their prayers. A million causes beg for our financial support. My wife and I have given to an organization which provides plastic surgery to children with extreme facial deformities. This organization is not specifically Christian; however, we believe it is a worthy cause and we receive joy by giving to it.

8. Good stewards are careful not to contribute to evil.

A few years ago, a certain hamburger chain started promoting their product with barely clothed young women simulating a sexual response while eating a burger. Even though I think this hamburger chain makes one of the best

---

[7] https://nccs.urban.org/project/nonprofit-sector-brief

hamburgers in the world, I decided I would no longer purchase their product. I have a wife, three daughters, and a son, and I want them to know I won't give my money to any business that exploits women. This shameless advertising promotes porn, gives men unrealistic expectations of women, makes the vast majority of the women in the world insecure about their bodies, and exposes young children to images they are too immature to process healthily. Matthew 16:26 says, "What profit is it to a man if he gains the whole world, and loses his own soul?" I believe this hamburger chain has given its soul for a profit.

Yes, we should not knowingly contribute to evil with our money, but wickedness is everywhere. I could probably find something corrupt about almost any business. While we cannot avoid every instance of immorality, we should at least be sensitive to it.

I believe Christians today have become numb to sin. Therefore, we are becoming less discerning when it comes to how and where we spend our money. Now, you may not have the same convictions I do about the hamburger commercial, but as a good steward, at least take a step closer to discernment. Where could your money be better spent? Is there a company that holds to Christian principles or at least family values?

In-N-Out Burger, a fast-food chain based in California, has printed Bible passages on cups, wrappers, and other packaging. Chick-fil-A management publicly proclaims their Bible-based views, even closing all of their restaurants on Sundays. Tyson Foods, Hobby Lobby, Interstate Batteries, and Forever 21 clothing stores are some of the many companies whose founders and/or owners publicly discuss their Christian faith. Personally, I would rather support companies like these than a burger chain that uses seductive commercials which exploit women to entice me to buy their products.

One word of warning in this area, though. Don't go to the opposite extreme and demand that everyone else adhere to your convictions. If you decide not to spend your money at a particular hamburger joint, don't judge those who do.

This was a problem in the first century too. The Pharisees tried to use legalism to trick Jesus. They asked Him, "Is it lawful for us to pay taxes to Caesar or not?"

> But He perceived their craftiness, and said to them, "Why do you test Me? Show Me a denarius. Whose image and inscription does it have?"
>
> They answered and said, "Caesar's."
>
> And He said to them, "Render therefore to Caesar the things that are Caesar's, and to God the things that are God's."
>
> Luke 20:22–25

During the first century, the Romans were doing many evil things with the money they received in taxes. Jesus did not condemn them for paying taxes. Instead, He told them to give to God what belongs to Him. We cannot dictate how the government or businesses spend the money we give to them. However, we should be discerning so we are not blindly contributing to evil.

9. Good stewards are humble.

First Timothy 6:17–19 says:

> Command those who are rich in this present age not to be haughty, nor to trust in uncertain riches but in the living God, who gives us richly all things to enjoy. Let them do good, that they be rich in good works, ready to give, willing to share, storing up for themselves a good foundation for the time to come, that they may lay hold on eternal life.

I have heard some wealthy Christians say that God has "blessed" them with money. In the next breath, they attribute their affluence to rugged individualism, risk-taking, great leadership, strength, personal fortitude. And they accept much praise from others.

If you don't have the right perspective, wealth can be a curse rather than a blessing. It can lead to pride, greed, pleasure-seeking, and unsatisfied ambition rather than a right relationship with God and love for your Christian brothers and sisters. For some it would be better to remain in poverty.

10. Good stewards give of themselves by serving in a local church.

Your pastor is not the only minister in the church. Every Christian is a full-time minister, whether paid by the church or not. Christ has called all of us to give of ourselves in service.

Church is a family, and in the context of any family, everyone needs to do chores that contribute to the health of the household. If only a few people are doing all the work in a local church, that church will not fare well.

The Bible uses a human body to illustrate this principle.

> Concerning spiritual gifts, brethren, I do not want you to be ignorant:
> ... There are diversities of gifts, but the same Spirit. There are differences of ministries, but the same Lord. And there are diversities of activities, but it is the same God who works all in all. But the manifestation of the Spirit is given to each one for the profit of all . . . .
> For as the body is one and has many members, but all the members of that one body, being many, are one body, so also is Christ . . . .
> For in fact the body is not one member but many.
> If the foot should say, "Because I am not a hand, I am not of the body," is it therefore not of the body? And if the ear should say, "Because I am not an eye, I am not of the body," is it therefore not of the body? If the whole body were an eye, where would be the hearing? If the whole were hearing, where would be the smelling? But now God has set the members, each one of them, in the body just as He pleased. And if they were all one member, where would the body be?

But now indeed there are many members, yet one body. And the eye cannot say to the hand, "I have no need of you"; nor again the head to the feet, "I have no need of you." No, much rather, those members of the body which seem to be weaker are necessary. And those members of the body which we think to be less honorable, on these we bestow greater honor; and our unpresentable parts have greater modesty, but our presentable parts have no need. But God composed the body, having given greater honor to that part which lacks it, that there should be no schism in the body, but that the members should have the same care for one another. And if one member suffers, all the members suffer with it; or if one member is honored, all the members rejoice with it.

Now you are the body of Christ, and members individually.

1 Corinthians 12:1, 4-7, 12, 14-27

The main teaching of this passage: We need each other, and everyone has to contribute in service in some way. We must all be involved in the churches we attend. That may mean being involved in leadership, vision, and development. Or making sure the trash cans are emptied and the chairs get placed back in order after every gathering. The Holy Spirit determines our chores, so we must pay attention to His direction for what He wants us to do and give.

11. Good stewards allow others to give to them.

Sometimes accepting is harder than giving. I learned this lesson thirty-five years ago. When I went to the house of an older friend, he often offered me something to eat or drink. I usually declined because, as I looked around his house, I could tell he did not have much money. I felt guilty for taking from him.

One day he told me I had offended him. Taken aback, I asked what he meant. He said, "In my culture, when someone offers you food or drink, you take it, whether you're hungry or not. It shows honor and respect. It says to your host that their offering is important and worthy. When you say no, you are communicating that you don't approve of their offering."

I had never thought of it that way.

Sometimes accepting blessings from friends is the most respectful thing you can do. It tells them they matter, that their offer is appreciated, that you love them, and their gift is valuable. If you are struggling financially, don't let pride stop you from letting others serve you.

Many people today are barely making ends meet. Spouses have passed away and single parents are raising children on their own. People are in the midst of a financial emergency because they lost a job, their car broke down, their house has gone down in value. Parents of college students are facing skyrocketing tuition. Retired people are trying to live on Social Security. Is *everybody* required to give, even when they can't afford it?

Those who are living in poverty or barely making it are not required to give any money to the church or other causes. The church should be giving to them. When passing the bucket, ushers should encourage them to take from what's there instead of making them feel guilty about not being able to add to it.

On the other hand, many times the Holy Spirit leads poor people to give money. Those who are poor are sometimes the most generous people in the church when it comes to helping others in need.

12. Some Christians have a divine gift of giving.

While we all should give, some Christians actually have a calling in this area. Their role within the church is as important as a pastor's calling to preach the Word of God.

> Having then gifts differing according to the grace that is given to us, let us use them: if prophecy, let us prophesy in proportion to our faith; or ministry, let us use it in our ministering; he who teaches, in teaching; he who exhorts, in exhortation; *he who gives, with liberality*; he who leads, with diligence; he who shows mercy, with cheerfulness.
>
> Romans 12:6–8 (emphasis added)

The Greek word for "giving" here is *metadidōmi*. It is a compound word meaning "to share or impart" (*meta* means "with"; *didōmi* means "to give")[8]. The same word is used in Luke 3:11:

---

8 *Vine's Complete Expository Dictionary of Old and New Testament Words* (Nashville: Thomas Nelson Publishers, 1996)

> He answered and said to them, "He who has two tunics, let him *give* to him who has none; and he who has food, let him do likewise" (emphasis added).

It is also used in Ephesians 4:28:

> Let him who stole steal no longer, but rather let him labor, working with his hands what is good, that he may have something to *give* him who has need (emphasis added).

This word has a deeper sense than just giving something you own to someone else. It means sharing something with someone while at the same time retaining possession of it. In a sense, you own it together. It is used in this sense when we impart the gospel to someone. We share the good news of salvation, but we keep our portion as well.

Many years ago my car broke down. Without blinking an eye, my friend Pete twisted a key off his key ring and handed it to me. He told me to take his extra car and use it as long as I needed. Pete is not wealthy. He and his wife, Kim, were planning to sell that extra car for needed cash. But he temporarily put off his financial reward for a brother in need. That is true *metadidōmi*.

Romans 12 goes on to say that he who gives should do so liberally. Some people interpret this as giving a large amount. However, this word means to share without any strings attached.

When I was a kid, my mother made my little sister share a cookie with me. My sister held out the cookie, but she wouldn't let go. As I tried to wrestle it away from her, it crumbled and fell to the ground. We both cried. But then she smiled in victory, as if she preferred seeing the cookie tossed into the garbage over letting me enjoy even a portion of it.

Before you think I'm throwing my sister under the bus, I too am guilty of giving things to people I didn't really want to let go of. I did so reluctantly. That is the opposite of *metadidōmi*.

Giving or sharing sacrificially is a specific gift given by the Holy Spirit to certain members of the body of Christ. While every believer should be generous with his or her money and possessions, some people go beyond generous.

Some very wealthy people have this special gift. They may contribute large amounts of money to a church vision. Or establish a trust fund with the money they will leave behind upon their death to fund hospitals, treatment centers, missionary organizations, or church plants. Others set up philanthropic organizations that fund multiple Christian organizations. In many instances, few people know who they are.

Many middle-class and even poor people possess this gift too. They have no problem sharing what they own with others, with no strings attached.

My good friend Anna makes her living by selling homemade fabric flowers and other crafts at a flea market. She doesn't make a lot of money. But every Tuesday, she and a number of others from her church gather in her kitchen to prepare delicious meals and bring them to the Mexican border, where they feed the homeless and share the gospel.

THE CHEERFUL GIVER

Is this tithing? No. She is listening to the Holy Spirit, doing what she can with what God has provided her for the week. And her reward in heaven will be great.

CHAPTER FIVE

Grace to Those Who Differ

Perhaps your pastor or other member of your church has a different view on the subject of tithing and giving. Please do not use this book to confront the leadership of your church on this issue. Confrontation, when not done humbly or prayerfully, can be damaging to relationships. It puts the other person on the defense. There is a better way.

The information contained in this book is for your personal use, as a starting point for your own study of what the Bible teaches about giving today. We should not be fighting among ourselves about money. Yes, we should be ready to give an account as to why we hold the position we do. However, it is not your responsibility to change everyone's mind. First of all, you *can't*. And second, it's not worth it. You'll only start an argument and you could get labeled as a troublemaker. In all things we are to love one another, whether we agree with them or not.

Second Timothy 2:23–25 says:

> Avoid foolish and ignorant disputes, knowing that they generate strife. And a servant of the Lord must not quarrel but be gentle to all, able to teach, patient, in humility correcting those who are in opposition, if God perhaps will grant them repentance, so that they may know the truth.

Titus 9:9–11 says:

> Avoid foolish disputes, genealogies, contentions, and strivings about the law; for they are unprofitable and useless. Reject a divisive man after the first and second admonition, knowing that such a person is warped and sinning, being self-condemned.

Our goal is not to be right; it is to love one another. We are all learning. We are all disciples. Even pastors. Pray for them as they dive into the Word every week, that they would be faithful and consistent in their teaching, always presenting the truth accurately. When they get it right, rejoice and learn. If occasionally they get something wrong, extend grace. And to the best of your ability, be faithful to your own calling. A better way of helping someone have a better understanding of the Bible is to start a simple conversation. Perhaps begin with a question and allow the Holy Spirit to do His work. Gently challenge the other person to look at the context of the tithing passages, follow up and see if their position changes.

Some pastors and teachers continue to follow the cultural practices of the patriarchal age and the instruction of the Mosaic law, which the church is no longer under. Others teach tithing out of tradition. Don't let this be a divisive issue. We must all individually seek truth.

Bibliography

Croteau, David, Bobby Eklund, Ken Hemphill, Reggie Kidd, Gary North, and Scott Preissler, *Perspectives on Tithing: 4 Views*. Nashville: B&H Publishing Group, 2011.

Durant, Will. *The History of Civilization, vol. 1: Our Oriental Heritage*. New York: Simon and Schuster, 1935.

Josephus, Flavius, "Antiquities of the Jews," in *Josephus: The Complete Works*. Translated by William Whiston. Tennessee: Thomas Nelson Publishers, 1998.

The New Unger's Bible Dictionary. Chicago: Moody Bible Institute, 1988.

Quiggle, James D. *Why Christians Should Not Tithe*. Eugene: Wipf and Stock Publishers, 2009.

Ramsey, Dave. *Money Matters* video study, Session 4: Giving. https://www.youtube.com/watch?v=daArgZ923YA.

Ramsey, Dave. *Dave Ramsey's Financial Peace University Workbook*. Brentwood: The Lampo Group, 2008.

Searcy, Nelson. *The Generosity Ladder*. Grand Rapids: Baker Books, 2010.

www.ingramcontent.com/pod-product-compliance
Lightning Source LLC
Chambersburg PA
CBHW031416040426

42444CB00005B/595